This book is dedicated to:

_____

(Name of Child)

Dream big and grow up to be
anything you want to be!

First Printing

ISBN Hardcover: 978-1-7342218-9-3

Illustrated by Amina Yaqoob

Printed in the United States of America

Clark and Hill Enterprise, LLC

6655 Santa Barbara Rd, #8681

Elkridge, MD 21075

www.clarkandhillenterprise.com

www.iamdrpgurley.com

Brown Boy, Break Barriers

When you grow up, Brown Boy, Be AMBITIOUS.

You can be anything and everything you want to be.

2

Brown Boy, Be a LANDSCAPER.

Design a paradise in the backyard with fountains, flowers, gazebos, and ponds.

Brown Boy, Be a THERAPIST.

Listen and help people with their thoughts, manners, and feelings.

6

Brown Boy, Be a HOCKEY PLAYER.

Skate and dangle and score on the ice, then score some more.

Brown Boy, Be a FIGURE SKATER.

**Shimmer, spin, glide, and
twist around an ice rink
as if no one was there.**

Brown Boy, Be a PROPFESSIONAL RACE CAR DRIVER.

Drive fast on the race track, past other race cars, and win your trophy.

Brown Boy, Be a BALLET DANCER.

Leap, stretch, and extend,
and lift beautiful ballerinas
on the stage.

Brown Boy, Be a JUDGE.

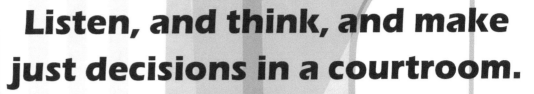

Listen, and think, and make just decisions in a courtroom.

Brown Boy, Be a FASHION DESIGNER.

Cut, sew, and measure knits, prints, denim, and faux leather in your unique style for the runway.

Brown Boy, Be a VETERINARIAN.

Aid and check animals big and small so they can play and be healthy.

Brown Boy, Be an ACCOUNTANT.

Add and count and calculate
to help others budget their money.

Brown Boy, Be a REAL ESTATE AGENT.

**Visit homes large and small
and new and old to sell or buy
for families to own.**

24

BROWN Boy, BE A Farmer.

25

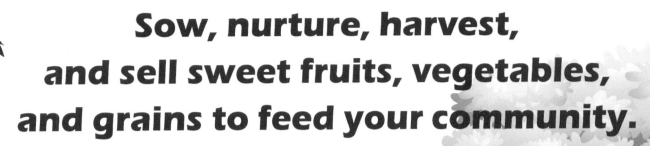

Sow, nurture, harvest,
and sell sweet fruits, vegetables,
and grains to feed your community.

Brown Boy,
Be a COMPETITVE SWIMMER.

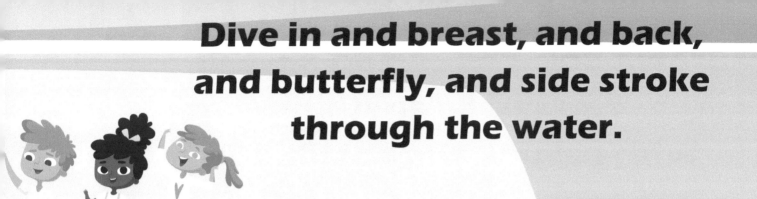

Dive in and breast, and back, and butterfly, and side stroke through the water.

28

So, without doubt or hesitation...
Brown Boy, BREAK BARRIERS.

About the Author

Professional Speaker and Author, Dr. Pamela Gurley is the founder and CEO/Founder of @clarkandHillEnterprise, CEO/Founder of IamDrPGurley; CEO/Founder of Un@apologeticbyDrG @unapologeticbydrg), CEO/Founder of D.A.W. Entertainment, Contributing Author of "Living A Non-Negotiable Lifestyle: My Life + My Dream + My Ambition = My Success"; Adjunct Graduate School Professor; Founder and Host of Herspiration Happy Hour podcast; Host of Vlog Series Un@pologetic w/ DrG; Editor/Contributing Writer for We Empower (WE) and Hustle & Soul Magazine.

Dr. Pam has been featured in Forbes and Hype Magazine; as well as, on Good Morning Washington (abcDC7), Good Day Atlanta (Fox5Atl), The Quiet Storm w/ Lenny Green, The Book of Sean (FoxSoul), Hot914 Radio, Fox34, NBC, CBS, and many other media outlets.

She is a retired United States Army Veteran and holds a Bachelor of Arts in Psychology from Saint Leo University; a Master's in Health Service Administration from Central Michigan University; and a Doctorate in Management with a concentration in Organizational Development and Change from Colorado Technical University.

Other books by author

1. I am Not a Stereotype: I Am H.E.R.
2. Bl@ck Girl Activist: Changing the Narrative for Black Women

Other books in series:

3. Brown Boy Be Social
4. Brown Girl, Be Social
5. Brown Girl, Break Barriers

CPSIA information can be obtained
at www.ICGtesting.com
Printed in the USA
LVHW072003270921
698834LV00002BA/8